BRITAIN IN OL.

BRIERLEY HILL

STAN HILL

ALAN SUTTON PUBLISHING LIMITED

Alan Sutton Publishing Limited
Phoenix Mill · Far Thrupp · Stroud
Gloucestershire · GL5 2BU

First published 1995
Reprinted with corrections 1996

Copyright © Stan Hill, 1995

Cover photographs: (front) Harold Thompson,
1962; (back) Brierley Hill town ambulance.
Title page: Free Library and Technical
Institute, built 1903.

British Library Cataloguing in Publication Data.
A catalogue record for this book is available
from the British Library.

ISBN 0–7509–1164–6

Typeset in 9/10 Sabon.
Typesetting and origination by
Alan Sutton Publishing Limited.
Printed in Great Britain by
WBC Limited, Bridgend.

Brierley Hill's coat of arms was assigned to the Council by letters patent dated 19 June 1942. The Arms combine representations of the local industries and the Arms of King's Swineford (Kingswinford). The glass, iron, steel and fireclay industries are denoted by the two beacons. The boars' heads are the 'King's Swine', and the two circles in the centre with wavy lines represent the fords adjoining the ancient manor of 'Suinesford' by which swine crossed from the manor to the wastelands beyond. The rose represents the briar rose which used to abound on the hill from which the district derived its name. The knot is the Stafford Knot. The motto is *'Sine labore nihil floret'* – 'Without labour nothing flourishes'.

Contents

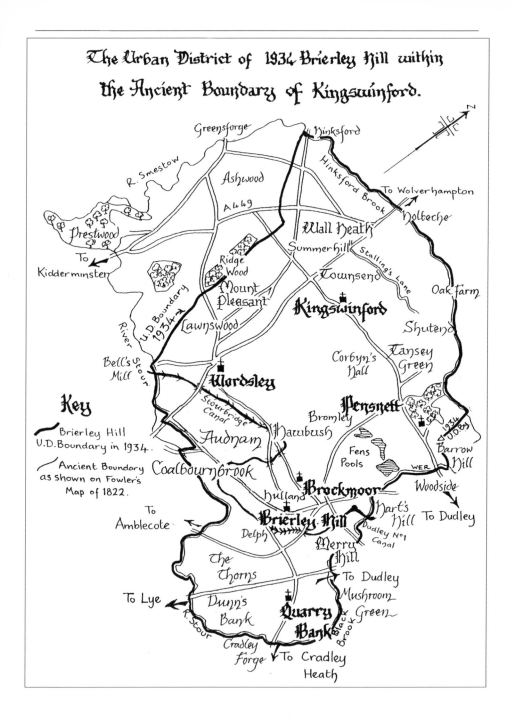

The Urban District of 1934 Brierley Hill within the Ancient Boundary of Kingswinford.

Introduction

What became Brierley Hill Urban District as a result of the 1934 Staffordshire Review Order, when the former urban districts of Brierley Hill and Quarry Bank and the rural district of Kingswinford amalgamated, roughly coincided with the ancient parish of Kingswinford and the Chase of Pensnett.

The rough scrubland hill in the middle of the Chase was first noted as a settlement in Kingswinford Manor's Court Rolls of 1619. Then, as it had been from time immemorial, it was open wasteland, part of Pensnett Chase with its laws and enforcement officers, Chief Ranger, foresters and coney keepers, all responsible to the lord of the manor.

Before the Conquest the manor of Kingswinford had come into the king's hands. About the year AD 1000, King Ethelred sold it to the Dean of Worcester, and after the death of Harold it came into King William's hands. In the Domesday Survey of 1068 the Staffordshire entry for the manor is 'Suinesford', and it is also recorded under Worcestershire as 'Svinesforde'.

From 1205 the lords of the manor were the de Somerys, the Suttons and Wards. The Chase was hunting country for parties from Dudley Castle. A 1272 survey of Kingswinford Manor refers to a wood at Pennack, probably that which covered the northern and southern slopes of the 'brierley hill' which joined up with Saltwells Wood. Pennack became Penned, Pensenytt, Pinsnett and finally Pensnett.

Originally the Chase covered an area extending as far as Enville and Bobbington, but the boundaries were vague and they contracted as more and more ground was taken and cultivated. However, the River Stour was a clear boundary dividing the Chase from the manor of Cradley. Also clear were tenants' holdings which abutted the lord's waste.

By the 16th century villages had already developed at Wordsley, Bredhull (Brettell), Bromley, Shut End, Brierley Hill and Quarry Bank, 'liberties' within the parish of Kingswinford. In the late 18th and early 19th centuries Brierley Hill and Quarry Bank grew rapidly.

The parish of Kingswinford was unchanged for almost 1,000 years and there had been a church at the northern end since the late 11th century. It is known that a priest lived there in 1186, and a record of 1199 mentions the church and its parson, William Spencer, Rector. It was at this time that the place became 'Swinford Regis' perhaps to distinguish it from 'Swinford Vetus', Old Swinford. From the Middle Ages population growth accelerated in the settlements away from the old village, and steps were taken by the Church to meet the new conditions.

For centuries various bodies and their appointees had administered local affairs. These functioned from the church vestry and the lord of the manor's courts. The rector of Kingswinford appointed churchwardens and overseers of the poor whose meetings were held in St Mary's Church vestry, and in the 18th and 19th centuries sometimes in the workhouse or schoolroom.

The manorial courts, the Court Baron and the Court Leet, were held in one of the district's larger houses, for example Corbyn's Hall, Ashwood Lodge and Turn Croft. In later years meetings were held in Lord Dudley and Ward's Court House, which still stands on the main road opposite Kingswinford village and church. The last official meetings were held in 1850. Some of the officials recorded were lord's steward, biddle, reeve, forester, ranger, constable, thirdborough and aletaster.

In the 19th century the Vestry at Brierley Hill was also involved with postal services and even, in 1847, discussion about the site of the railway station to serve the growing population of Brierley Hill and Brockmoor, for whom that built at Round Oak was inconvenient. In 1851 there was a Lighting Committee, and after the Local Government Act of 1867 a local Board of Health was appointed, which concerned itself with the provision of a water supply. This was later undertaken by the South Staffordshire Waterworks Company.

For more than 600 years St Mary's Church at Kingswinford was the only place of worship, but by the end of the 18th century it was inadequate for a parish which was rapidly increasing in population away from its ancient site. This, and because it was thought to be in danger from advancing mining operations, led to its closure and the opening of Holy Trinity Church, Wordsley, as a replacement mother church with accommodation for 1,500, in 1831.

To meet the growing needs of the Brierley Hill district, some 4 miles south-east, the chapel, St Michael's, was built at Brierley Hill and consecrated in 1765.

During the incumbency of the Revd George Saxby Penfold at Holy Trinity (1832–46) the ancient parish was divided into six, each with its own parish church: Wordsley (1831), Brierley Hill (1842), Brockmoor (1845), Quarry Bank (1845), Kingswinford (recommissioned 1848) and Pensnett (1849). Quarry Bank, Brockmoor and Pensnett were new churches.

There were several mission churches. At Harts Hill a Dissenters' chapel was purchased in 1838 and became a chapel of ease to Brierley Hill, transferring to St Augustine's Church, Holly Hall, in 1930. At the Delph, in the midst of fireclay mining operations, the Church of the Good Shepherd was built in 1886. It accommodated 400 and there was also a 400-strong Sunday School. By 1914 it was in a dilapidated state and public figures were calling for its repair. It was demolished in 1952.

At Bromley, in 1869, a mission church was built of wood and corrugated iron, and from 1929 this was run by a Church Army evangelist. The church no longer exists.

Before the 1870 Education Act there were several 'Dame Schools'. National schools under Church of England control were established in Brierley Hill (1835), Quarry Bank (1845), Brockmoor (1846) and Pensnett (1861).

Methodist church accommodation was also used for classes. Board schools were built at Brierley Hill (1882), Brockmoor (1887), and Quarry Bank (Mount Pleasant, 1888); the last was modernised and is still in use.

The year 1888 saw the establishment of Staffordshire County Council, and in 1894 district divisions of the county, urban districts and rural districts, were carved out of the huge county authority to administer minor local services. Amblecote, originally a ward of Kingswinford Rural District, became an urban district, and successfully resisted being included in the 1934 amalgamations – and remained so until incorporated in a slightly larger Stourbridge Municipal Borough in 1966. The other three old 1894 districts became Brierley Hill Urban District.

By 1939 the enlarged Brierley Hill Urban District had become an effective unit and great progress was made in several fields, particularly slum clearance and the building of council houses. The Second World War, with all the additional duties imposed upon local authorities by the Government, further strengthened Brierley Hill Council. Such was the pride and confidence of Brierley Hill UDC in the late 1940s that early in the 1950s great efforts were made to achieve borough status. A petition was presented to the privy council for Brierley Hill to be incorporated as a municipal borough. A public enquiry was held and there was great support from local industry, commerce, local organisations and the public. Hopes were raised when another Midlands urban district, Solihull, which had petitioned a little earlier, was granted municipal borough status in 1954. But it was not to be for Brierley Hill. Much more extensive local government reorganisation plans for the whole country were afoot.

When these became law in the mid-1960s the effect in the Black Country was the disappearance of some 20 minor local authorities, including Brierley Hill Urban District which became part of the enlarged county borough of Dudley. Amblecote, although in Staffordshire, was absorbed by the Worcestershire municipal borough of Stourbridge. In 1974 there were further changes when the boroughs of Stourbridge and Halesowen were absorbed into a further enlarged Dudley, designated a Black Country metropolitan borough. However, much local pride in the former townships remains, despite the local government and employment changes.

The bases for the rapid industrial development of the district were the South Staffordshire Coal Measures and the iron and fireclay deposits. There are 13th-century records of 'sea-coal' being extracted locally, and these mineral resources were exploited progressively from the Middle Ages, leading to the Chase becoming one of the earliest and busiest industrialised areas of the country. The Brierley Hill part became the biggest and the busiest in the developing region.

Ironstone was extracted in considerable quantities and smiths used charcoal to smelt it. Nailing developed at Wordsley and spread throughout the parish. Coal was extracted over both sides of the 'brierley hill', and the population increased tenfold to 1,500 between 1500 and 1600. These changes mark the beginning of the Industrial Revolution.

The increasing demand from the growing community for wood as fuel, and its shortage, led to the expansion of coal production. Dud Dudley, Lord Dudley's illegitimate son, claimed in 1665 to have smelted iron ore in the parish using coal instead of charcoal, but if he did so the secret was lost until Abraham Darby continued the process from 1709 at Coalbrookdale.

Coal was the attraction which brought the Lorraine glassmakers to the district, the de Hennezels, Thysacs, Thietrys and Houx, perhaps to build upon the rudimentary smelting of glass with the coal system already believed to be operating at Greensforge. By 1618 some of the Lorrainers' anglicised names were appearing in parish registers. Another attraction for them was fireclay. As this latter industry grew, large numbers of women were employed in it. It became known as Stourbridge fireclay and the glass industry became known as Stourbridge glass, as Stourbridge was the old-established nearby town with banking and accommodation facilities for dealers.

The growing population and the change from an agricultural to an industrial economy led to demands for quantities of food which could not be met by age-old methods. Enclosure of common wastes led to improved farming practices to produce the food necessary for the exploding population, which tripled nationally from 6 million in 1750 to 18 million in 1850. On the Chase two Acts of Parliament, in 1776 and 1784, covered the matter. By these acts the Lord Dudley Estate increased considerably in size and rights.

The difficulties in transporting the growing volume of raw materials and finished goods led to the spread of canals. The Staffordshire–Worcestershire Canal skirted the western boundary of the parish from the mid-1770s but little benefit resulted from it locally. This led to an Act of Parliament in 1776 authorising the cutting of a canal to link the Chase with the established canal at Stourton. This followed the Stour Valley east to Wordsley, up the Stourbridge 16 locks to Brockmoor, a sweep around Brierley Hill, under the old turnpike road at Brettell Lane and then to the Delph where it joined the Dudley Canal. The link to Dudley and the Birmingham canal system was by the Nine Locks to Park Head and the Dudley Tunnel. Many branch canals were cut from the Stourbridge and Dudley canals to ironworks, brickworks, mines and factories, and for 60 years local industry's expansion was aided greatly by this new form of inland bulk transport.

It is recorded that by this new system 32,000 tons of coal and 11,000 tons of other goods were conveyed from the Chase in 1798, and in 1824 the total amount of freight was 93,000 tons.

Local locomotive railways became established. The first opened in 1829 from Shut End pits to Ashwood Basin linked to the Staffordshire–Worcestershire Canal. The first locomotive, the *Agenoria*, was made by Messrs Foster, Rastrick and Co., at Amblecote on the Stourbridge branch. The locomotive worked on the line until 1860 and is now preserved in the National Railway Museum, York. This industrial line became known as the Pensnett Railway and had 40 miles of track linking the Earl of Dudley's enterprises.

The Oxford, Worcester and Wolverhampton Railway, started in 1845, was laid through the area and reached Wolverhampton in 1854. The line climbed from Stourbridge Junction through Brettell Lane, Brierley Hill and Round Oak, where it passed the New Level furnaces. From Brettell Lane, the

Kingswinford branch to Gornal and Himley was constructed between 1855 and 1859. By 1860 Brierley Hill was well served by canal and railway, and industry prospered.

Brierley Hill lies in that area where the 30 foot thick coal seam outcropped or lay up to 500 feet below the surface. This was extensively worked throughout the 19th century and at lower depths, later, on the periphery. In the 1960s, long after traditional mining had ceased in the area, coal was extracted in huge quantities by opencast mining in the Withymoor area, 8–10,000 tons weekly for about two years. The site later became an extensive housing estate, Withymoor Village. On the OS map of 1881–2 over 100 mines are marked in the Brierley Hill area alone.

Side by side with the exploitation of coal deposits went iron production. On the 1881–2 OS map numerous ironworks are marked; the most substantial and enduring, Round Oak Ironworks, was established in 1857 by the Dudley Estate on the site of the New Level Ironworks, previously operated by B. Gibbons. The new ironworks was twice the size of the average, employed 600 men, and from the time of its establishment until its demise in November 1982 was always expanding and improving. The works converted to steel production in 1892 and at its peak produced some 5 per cent of the nation's steel requirement and employed several thousand personnel. There were other producers of iron locally and very many users of it. The 1950 Brierley Hill and District Trades Association listed in their brochure some 20 manufacturers. Only three remain. Another big employer of labour which closed in the 1980s was Richard Thomas and Baldwins.

Round Oak Steelworks closed in 1982 and the 200 acre site was bought by two Brierley Hill entrepreneurs, Messrs Don and Roy Richardson, who have developed on it one of the biggest shopping and commercial centres in Europe, the Merry Hill Centre. This has had a considerable effect on neighbouring towns from which national chain stores have moved their businesses to Merry Hill. Brierley Hill, however, only a few hundred yards away, which only had one famous chain store, continues to thrive. The old manufacturers, employers of large labour forces, have gone. The Merry Hill complex is estimated to employ some 7,000 people, many of whom have simply transferred with their employers from other locations. A number of small manufacturers have started up, some on the several trading estates in the area.

The whole place is now much cleaner and greener than when it was a hive of heavy industry and more local people have to travel further to find work.

Despite all the difficulties, Brierley Hill people have responded with true Black Country spirit and determination to overcome adversities.

Brierley Hill developed rapidly in the 19th century between the Dudley–Stourbridge road running left to right in the centre of this 1950s aerial view, and the former GWR Worcester–Wolverhampton line near the bottom, with the station on the left and the signal box near to Moor Street bridge on the right. St Michael's Church (1765) served as a chapel of ease in the ancient parish of Kingswinford. The town was dominated by Round Oak Works, just off left centre, and Marsh and Baxter Ltd, to the left of St Michael's Church. Between the Old Level Works (part of Round Oak Works), top left, and Two Woods Lane, top right, Richardson Developments have, since 1982, built the Merry Hill Centre, one of the largest shopping and commercial centres in Europe. Marsh & Baxter Ltd was demolished in 1979 and the site became the Moor Shopping Centre. Most of the properties in the quadrilateral, centre left, have been demolished and new houses built.

BRIERLEY HILL

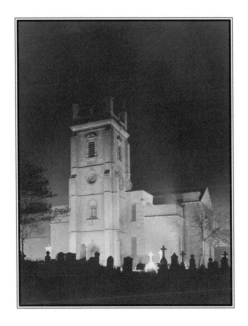

*St Michael's Church was consecrated in 1765 as
Brierley Hill Chapel. It was built to serve the
growing population around the higher part of the
ancient parish of Kingswinford. It became a
separate chapelry in 1842 and a separate parish
in 1848.*

This is how the interior of St Michael's Church will be remembered by many. The interior was redesigned to meet the changing needs of the church, and the relinquishing of the Church Hall to Dudley Metropolitan Borough for use as a community centre.

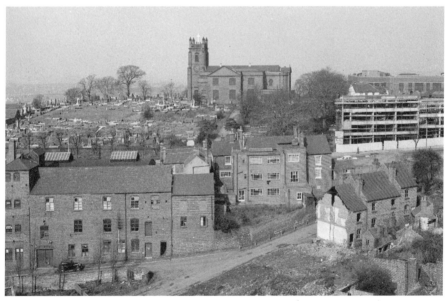

This view of the church is from the flats, 1965. On the right is Marsh & Baxter Ltd and the new shops development of Church Street. Derry Street is in the foreground, with New Street on the left running steeply down to Delph Road.

Delph Mission Church, dedicated in 1886, seated 400. By 1884 it was dilapidated but two world wars and lack of money thwarted rebuilding. It was taken down in 1952. Withymoor Village covers the site.

Harts Hill Mission Church was bought from Dissenters in 1838, to serve as an outpost to St Michael's Church for the growing population astride the boundary with Dudley. It was transferred to the parish of St Augustine, Holly Hall, in 1930 and demolished in the 1970s.

Bank Street Methodist Church opened on 11 October 1829 and cost £1,200; it survived early subsidence problems. A new £50,000 church to serve the members of several other Methodist churches which closed and have been demolished opened in 1971, free of debt. The photograph was taken just before demolition in 1969.

The interior of the original Bank Street Methodist Church.

Bank Street Methodist Church Guides and Rangers, *c.* 1944. Captain Norah Frost is on the extreme left and behind her Doreen Proctor, flag bearer. Lt. Ethel Hodgetts, Ranger Leader is centre, back row, and to her left is the Revd R.L. Brook, minister.

The interior of the Congregational Church, Albion Street, 1965. While the new Bank Street Methodist Church was being built, members of that church held their services here. Congregational Church members decided to join forces with the Methodists at Bank Street. The church is now used by the Assemblies of God, and the former schoolroom opposite by Jehovah's Witnesses.

This view from the Hill Street flats shows Round Oak Steelworks off Dudley Road, right, and Marsh & Baxter Ltd on the left, 1965. The Roman Catholic Church is in the centre and, below, St Michael's Church Hall is under construction on the site of the early 19th-century Church of England school.

Another view of the flats development in 1965, on a site honeycombed with shallow 18th- and 19th-century mine workings. Top left are the once familiar five Round Oak chimney-stacks, known to photographers as 'The Cunarder'. The construction at the bottom is Potter Court.

The completed Chapel Street flats, an impressive sight on the skyline when approached from Quarry Bank, late 1960s. The flats replaced many substandard houses in New Street, Hill Street, Chapel Street, Derry Street, South Street, Brick-kiln Street and Potter Street. Round Oak Steelworks is top centre, and Delph Road at the bottom.

An 1870 photograph of Round Oak Ironworks.

Round Oak Ironworks with the offices on Dudley Road, early 1890s. The works became the Earl of Dudley's Round Oak Iron and Steel Works in 1897.

The demolition of a chimney-stack at Round Oak, 1920s. Alterations, developments and improvements continued throughout the existence of the works right up to within two years of closure. A Queen's Award for Exports was made for the 1977–80 period and an £8 million improvement was planned in 1980, yet the works closed down in 1982.

Vernon Oliver, left, with Round Oak chain on which is painted 'UNBROKEN AT 350 TONS', early 1920s.

The crane department at Round Oak, 1935. On the back row, left, is Bill Green, and on the front row, left, Arthur Sharratt Snr, and extreme right, Arthur Sharratt Jnr.

Desurfacing a 4 ton ingot at Round Oak, early 1970s. Left to right: Stan Westwood, Bill Ives (shift foreman), Jack Harris.

Round Oak Steelworks from Pedmore Road, early 1960s. The Queen's Head Inn still stands and is now a night club.

Level Street, which now runs through the Merry Hill-Waterfront shopping and commercial complex, 1960s. Two sets of level crossings for the industrial railway serving the Earl of Dudley's pits and works can be seen. The large building is the new melting shop.

'The Cunarder', the five chimney-stacks to the open hearth furnaces near Dudley Road, at night, 1960s.

An aerial view of Round Oak Works, just before demolition in the early 1980s.

Even in the late 1960s farming
activities were being carried on
just a few hundred yards from
High Street.

Parkes's Chainworks, Parkes Street, *c.* 1870. This works had disappeared by the turn of
the century.

Bailey Pegg & Co. were described in trade directories as 'Engineers, ironfounders and manufacturers for the supply of cast iron, retorts, gas, water, steam and cable pipes etc.' In this photograph, c. 1890, workers from the fitting shop are seen with a selection of their products. The foundry was situated in Bull Street, near Brettell Lane railway station.

Long-established company Samuel Taylor & Sons, Brettell Lane, specialised in equipment for ships. These anchors for the *Canberra* (1961) were made there. The firm was also famous for supplying high tensile steel chain cables for the Royal Navy, and lifeboat davits and winches for such giant liners as Cunard's two *Queens*.

A view of Stevens & Williams (Royal Brierley) glass works from the newly opened Marsh Park, 1920s. The road on the left continued to Moor Lane via a railway crossing until North Street was opened. The house in front of the glass cone is Honeybourne, where the manager, John Northwood II (1870–1960), lived.

The family of John Northwood I (1836–1901), manager and artistic director of Stevens & Williams (1880–1901), 1900. The group includes: on the third row, John Northwood I (third from right), Carl Northwood (third from left) and Harry Northwood (second row, right).

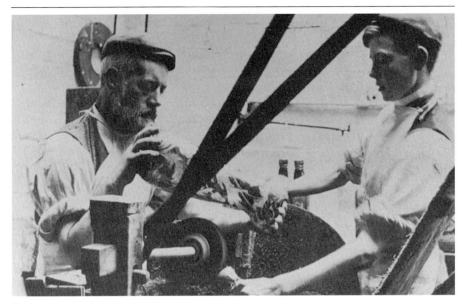

Frederick Carder, a schoolboy protégé of John Northwood I at the latter's own decorating works at Wordsley, joined Stevens & Williams as an apprentice glass designer in 1880. He emigrated in 1903 to the USA where he established the famous Steuben Glass Works, absorbed by Corning Glass Works in 1917, for whom he continued to work until he was 96 years of age. He died on 10 December 1963, aged 100 years.

Frederick Carder married Annie Walker of Dudley in 1887. They lived in John Street, Wordsley, and had three children: Stanley, who died in 1899 aged seven; Cyril, who was killed in action in France in 1918 while serving with the US Army; and Gladys, who survived into old age.

At the southern end of the town, in Hall Street, Marsh & Baxter's offices and works towered above the surrounding buildings. Founded in 1870 in Moor Street, the firm became one of the biggest meat processing factories in Europe, killing some 500 pigs each morning before 9 a.m. This photograph was taken in 1951.

Marsh & Baxter's new garage in Moor Street, early 1920s. It was built to house the growing fleet of delivery vehicles, over 50 at this time. The photograph shows a large open-cabbed wagon.

This 1932 Thornycroft truck with purpose-built coachwork by a West Bromwich firm was an improvement on the open-cab vehicles.

In 1930 Marsh & Baxter's works fire brigade attended a parade at Lye. Such brigades played an important role during the Second World War.

Marsh & Baxter closed down in December 1978, when the last 200 employees were made redundant. At one time over 1,800 people had been employed by the company, which was sold to the FMC. The demolition of the Brierley Hill works was the first major contract of successful local businessman, Anthony Whittaker.

This was a famous advertisement used before and after the Second World War; the catchphrase is said to have been coined by one of the workforce.

E.J. & J. Pearson's Delph Firebrick works, *c.* 1950, demolished in 1975. This view is from Delph Lock No. 7. Lock 8 (formerly 9) is against the road bridge and mainly obscured by the balance beams.

'Brickyard wenches', 1930s.

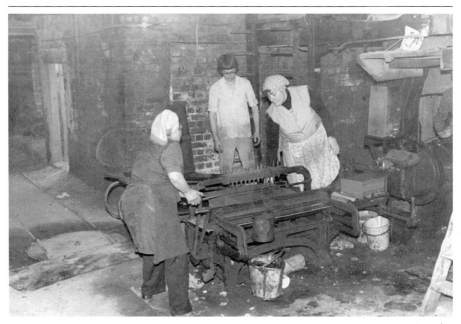

Until the 1950s women operated a simple cutting machine known as a 'pug' to cut bricks to the 9 × 4 × 3 inch dimensions from the block of malleable clay which emerged (above the bucket) from the mixing machine.

Brickyard workers made their own 'comforts' from scrap bricks and corrugated iron. This late 1940s shelter, known as the 'hovel', at E.J. & J. Pearson's, was equipped with discarded furniture from home, and used for tea and 'snap' breaks.

On 11 May 1963, 68-year-old Mrs Rachel Didlock of 32 Corbett Road received an award from Mr R.E.G. Evers (chairman of the Pearson Sub-Group of Price-Pearson Refractories) to mark her 50 years' service with the company. Starting in 1911, she worked for 12 hours a day for 12 to 15 shillings weekly. After marriage she brought up a family of four in addition to nursing a sick husband.

Plants Hollow mines and clay banks, 1920s. This was situated east of the railway line near to the 'Murder Bridge'. The higher track led to Crown Pit and that on the left to Brettell Lane, near the railway station.

Amblecote Works and mines, 1920s. The double track cable tramway carried clay to E.J. & J. Pearson's works.

Clay banks at Amblecote Pit, 1920s.

Amblecote No. 7 Pit, late 1960s. The weathered clay bank continued to be drawn upon after the pit ceased working.

Amblecote No. 7 Pit, with Batham's Vine Inn clearly seen between the two sets of steel headgear, late 1960s. The houses are on Delph Road.

Open-cast mining on the Withymoor site, late 1960s. Some 200 feet of overburden was removed to obtain the Thick Coal, 35 feet thick over some parts of this site. This had already been lightly mined since the 18th century. E.J. & J. Pearson's works is on the skyline.

Open-cast mining at Withymoor, with Bowen's brickworks on the Stourbridge Canal on the skyline, 1960s.

Nagersfield Colliery, 1920s. It belonged to George King Harrison, Firebrick Manufacturers, and was situated at the bottom of what is now Harrison Road. Coal and clay were extracted, and a rope tramway climbed to Brettell Lane and underneath it by tunnel to the works on the east side of Brettell Lane.

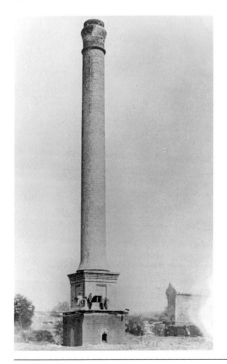

Preparations being made to demolish the Nagersfield Colliery chimney-stack, 1950s.

The chimney-stack after the explosion.

The explosion did not quite finish the job. Here the manager and staff discuss the next step.

An early 20th-century funeral procession, directed by Cartwright's, passes the Town Arms, demolished for road improvements in the 1960s. The space halfway along the row became the covered market. The sheep were probably being driven to the Albion Street saleyard. In front of a double-decker tram is a water cart.

The Elms, situated at the junction of High Street and Bank Street, early 20th century. On the death of the owners, the Misses Harris, whose family had owned firebrick works and had donated the almshouses in Seagers Lane, the property was acquired and demolished by Brierley Hill Urban District Council, and the Civic Centre developed on the site.

The Turk's Head, opposite The Elms, early 20th century. The inn offered waiting rooms for tram passengers, and good stabling for horse owners.

High Street from the top of Talbot Street (Dog Lane), near The Elms, early 20th century. The lady in the road is thought to be the housekeeper at The Elms. Note the Town Hall clock and double track tram lines.

A post-First World War ox-roast, with well-known High Street pork butcher, Fred Knott, in attendance.

The George Mason grocery shop, near Five Ways, c. 1920. Fifth from right is Selina (Linny) Harris, later Roberts; on the left is Bert Harris, later manager of Brockmoor Co-op. The Mason chain, founded in 1909, grew to be a national multiple of over 500 shops, and most Black Country towns had one.

High Street from Five Ways, looking towards the post office with PC Challinor on duty, late 1920s. On the left is the Five Ways Inn, and on the right what became the Horse Shoe Hotel, and next the Palace Theatre.

From a small clothing and home fabric shop founded in 1910, Chattin & Horton expanded into a substantial store with premises running back to Cottage Street. An extension sale was held in 1958 after adjacent property had been acquired. The store closed in April 1976: five long-serving staff had an average of 34 years service with the firm.

Derelict properties on the corner of Bell Street and Church Street just before their replacement by smart shops in the mid-1960s. The latter can be seen under construction in the lower photograph on page 12.

The approach to High Street from Silver End, 1980. The licensed premises, the New Inn and the Red Lion, had prevented Marsh & Baxter extending their premises to the main road, but the properties between had been acquired and demolished.

W.M. Richardson's High Street shop, 1910. Note the wide range of goods on sale and the gas lighting.

The premises of Boddenham & Co. in High Street, 1910. Established in the 1870s, this was another well-stocked shop.

Brierley Hill post office and police station, High Street, 1905. The curiously shaped building in the centre of the picture gave public access to the police court, on the front of which was a drinking fountain presented by the Local Board of Health in 1868.

The drinking fountain, seen here in its original position by the police station, was sculpted by William Griffiths who had a yard in Level Street and a shop in High Street. The fountain is now situated near the Moor Centre on High Street. This photograph, dating from 1978, shows Councillor Mrs Rosa Dangerfield and local historian Ernest Quinton, who were keen to save the relic.

M.A. Griffiths' shop, 1905, between Reads and the post office. The plaque reads: 'Established 1857, W. Griffiths & Son, Ornamental Sculptors'.

Another photograph of Griffiths' shop with Mrs Griffiths, right, and her 'domestic', Keziah Luciana Tomlinson, on the left, early 20th century. Norah Griffiths is the child on the left, and her brother Ronald is on the right.

High Street from the junction with Hill Street, *c.* 1960, by which time the properties were in a bad state. On the corner is Batham's Spread Eagle Inn; the narrow entrance to Chapel Street can just be seen together with four shops, and beyond, the Roman Catholic Church.

The properties next to the Spread Eagle Inn, High Street, 1914.

The Misses L. and A. Nicholson ran a ladies' and children's wear shop at 161 High Street opposite the Odeon Cinema, seen here in the 1930s. Note the large range of items including those on the first floor.

Shops near the Level Street junction with High Street, c. 1914. There seems to have been an incident, as a crowd of bystanders and a policeman are in attendance.

The Bright Home Stores, Mill Street, near the junction with Cottage Street, *c.* 1930. The business belonged to Thomas Lowther (centre), his brother Harry and their sister Norah (on Thomas's left). Late on Saturdays Mr Harbourne (right) toured butchers' shops to collect waste fat for the firm's candle factory in Addison Road.

The shops opposite the Bright Home Stores, 1979. The shops and Horse Shoe Hotel opposite the Mill Street entrance were demolished in the early 1980s and replaced by the Moor Centre.

Shops in Fenton Street near its junction with Moor Street, left, 1950s. The tall building on the left is Trembath's general store on the corner of Parkes Street. All were within the redevelopment site.

Mid-19th century cottages in Moor Street, 1950s. These were situated beyond the canal bridge near Addison Road and were demolished under a redevelopment scheme.

The early 19th-century cottages which stood in Dudley Road just beyond the Bank Street entrance, 1890s. In one of them, Mr Roberts of Roberts and Cooper, ironfounders, brickworks, mines and ship operators was born. The cottages were demolished in about 1900, and the Liberal Club was erected on the site.

The Liberal Club opened in 1902. It has been converted to another use, and the stones laid by supporters have been plastered over.

New Street, 1960s. Batham's Spread Eagle Inn is on the corner of High Street and Hill Street. The whole area was cleared in the 1960s for the building of multi-storey flats. The development was difficult because of the extensive early 19th-century shallow mining under the area.

The Laurels in Pearson Street had been the home of Ebenezer E. Cooper, a partner in Roberts and Cooper's ironworks at Brockmoor, and later of E.E.J. Roberts who operated a sawmill and timber business at Nine Locks until his death in 1925. The building became the Labour Club after 1925 and has been much altered.

Brick-kiln Street, 1960. This was part of the flats' redevelopment area behind the Roman Catholic Church in the 1960s.

These late Victorian houses in Bank Street are opposite the MEB station. The plaque states: 'One Man's Property – Erected 1891'.

Devastation was caused to the houses in Adelaide Street at 3.30 a.m. on 16 March 1944, when a damaged Halifax Mk 3 bomber No. LW413, returning from a massive raid on Germany, crashed. Mrs Bessie Rowbottom (32), staying the night at her parents' home, was killed.

Adelaide Street, the morning of the aircraft crash: seven houses were severely damaged and over 60 others were affected. The emergency services rescued several trapped residents and prevented fire spreading.

A small general shop in Dudley Road, 1954.

An early 19th-century cottage off Mill Street affected by mining subsidence, 1950.

Looking down Rocks Hill, which linked Hill Street with Delph Road, late 1940s. E.J. & J. Pearson's fire-brick works is by the canal bridge; Mrs Reynolds' house is on the left; Molly Hill lived in the house below and sold coal. Beyond is Withymoor, a source of clay and coal from the early 18th century.

Situated at the entrance to Brierley Hill from Dudley, Harts Hill bus garage was originally an electric tramway depot that dated back to the 1890s. From 1925 the premises were used by the Midland Red Motor Omnibus Company, and were extended in 1931 to accommodate 58 vehicles. This 1953 photograph shows a couple checking Coronation week coach excursions.

Church Street, looking south, 1956. In front of the war memorial on Church Hill is a cannon made by Bailey Pegg of Bull Street, and said to be like the one used by Baden Powell's force at the Siege of Mafeking (1900).

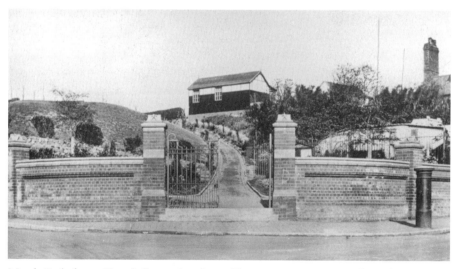

Marsh Park from Church Street, bowls pavilion centre, 1930s. On the right is a First World War tank, which was removed for scrap during the Second World War.

In 1894 the newly created Brierley Hill Urban District absorbed the functions of the Local Board of Health, which had been established in 1867. These two wooden panels are on the walls of the stairs in the Civic Buildings. There were nine further chairmen until 1966, when the urban district was absorbed by Dudley County Borough.

Councillors and officials of Brierley Hill Urban District Council, 1937. Back row, left to right: V.S. Pardoe, R.H.J. Comber, A. Workman, H. Edwards, F. Jones, A.F. White, E. Mantom, T. Whorton, C.F. Moore, H.J. Parker, L. Dixon. Second row: A.L. Titterington, J.T. Higgs, W. Shaw, F.A. Williams, T. Price, D. Guttery, B. Ryder, E.E. Marsh, H. Haden, H. Hex, E.W. Turner. Front row: R.H. Wood, J.B. Hill, J.P. Solari, W.J. Woodhall, J. Foxall, Dr Appleton, Mrs F. Hodgetts, T. Williams (chairman), Miss G. Rutledge, H. Hough, F. Oakes, S. Wood, J.N. Hickman.

The Town Hall was built in 1874, and besides being a public hall housed the early council offices and free library. It became known as the Queen's Hall and was used as a cinema until the late 1930s, and during the war as an ARP training centre.

The hall's interior as illustrated on a brochure of hire rates, 1900. It was last used in 1963 and demolished in 1968. In the redevelopment Brierley Hill Library was included on the first floor of the new building next to the Midland Bank.

Bringing up the rear of the parade for the Civic Service, 19 June 1955: Cllr Eric Gibbons (vice-chairman), Alderman Mrs Beatrice Simmons (Birmingham), C. James Simmons MP, Herbert Hex (clerk to the council), Mrs J.M. Hill and Cllr A.S. Hill (chairman).

In 1854, 24 miners and their families emigrated from Brierley Hill to Nanaimo, Vancouver Island, British Columbia, on Hudson's Bay Company contracts. In 1954 contact with Brierley Hill by the descendants of the emigrants was re-established for their centenary celebrations. In 1955 Mr R.J. Walley, vice-president of the Nanaimo Historical Society with his wife and sister, were received by the author, then chairman of the council, and given a guided tour of the district.

Councillor David Brookes JP, chairman of the council, laid the foundation stone of Brierley Hill baths, Cottage Street, in January 1960.

Councillor Tom Wells JP took the salute at a parade along High Street, 1966.

Councillor J.N. Hickman JP, chairman of the newly created Brierley Hill Urban District Council 1934–6, reading the Royal Proclamation following the death of King George V, from a rostrum erected outside the Queen's Hall (later Town Hall).

Declaration of the poll for the new Brierley Hill Constituency, February 1950. Left to right: Superintendent Hodnett, Mrs Dudley Williams, Dudley Williams (Con.), Herbert Hex (Deputy Acting Returning Officer), T.P. Hanley (Lib.), C.J. Simmons MP, Alderman Mrs Beatrice Simmons (Birmingham).

Brierley Hill Volunteer Fire Brigade parading to St Michael's Church, 1930s. Left to right: Captain Walker (elderly, heavy moustache, representing Stourbridge Fire Brigade), Eb. Beckley (front), Josiah Gordon, Captain Pargeter (Brierley Hill Brigade, right). Buildings, left to right: Market Hall, Market Vaults, Chattin & Horton, George Mason Grocery, Town Arms.

A fireman's wedding, c. 1930. There was great camaraderie among volunteer firemen. The rules included a 2s 6d fine for failure to turn out. The bridal pair are Wilfred and Irene Higgs; the firemen are, left to right, Captain Pargeter, Driver Cliff Murray, Eb. Beckley, and, to the left of the bride, Dan Simpkiss.

A 'civic baptism' of the new Urban District Council ambulance, mid-1930s. Driver Frank Beckley, councillors, officials and St Michael's Church Choir are shown. The Town Hall ground floor had been adapted to garage the fire engines.

Town Hall staff, *c.* 1925. Left to right: Kathy Clarke, Ike Fletcher, Mrs Lamb.

Round Oak railway station in Dudley Road, 1930s. This opened after the construction of the Oxford, Worcester and Wolverhampton Railway, which passed through in 1852. The booking office was at road level and access to the platforms was by a bridge and steps.

A Wolverhampton to Stourbridge passenger train at Brettell Lane station, the next stop south from Brierley Hill, 11 June 1962. A few hundred yards to the north was a branch to Oxley Junction via Wombourne.

Looking south, this passenger train pulls out of Brierley Hill station, 2 May 1957. To the left of the locomotive is the 'Stallage', a wooden platform construction built for use by Marsh & Baxter Ltd, in about 1927. Goods for South Wales were loaded into a rail van dropped off at 10.25 a.m., and collected by the 4.26 p.m. Stourbridge train.

A southbound freight train passes through Brierley Hill, 26 April 1961. The station opened in 1858 and passenger services ceased on 30 July 1962. The station was demolished in 1968. The road facing the line is West End, now Bradleymore Road.

The Nine Locks on Dudley No. 1 Canal from Mill Street Bridge, 1981. The line of the canal was altered in 1857, reducing the number of locks to eight. The handsome bridge was made by the Horseley Company in 1858. The stables on the left of the second lock down (No. 3) have been restored for community use.

The Nine Locks system from near the Bottom Lock, 1975.

The Notice of Closure on the gate pillars of Bent Street (actually in John Street) Infants' School, 1972. The school in the background is Bent Street Board School, which opened in 1882.

A class at Bent Street Board School before reorganisation, 1930. Back row, left to right: Cathy Carter, Peggy Maw, -?-, Kathleen Wood, Phyllis Sharratt, Peggy Scott, -?-, Gwen Lindsey, -?-, Eileen Hill. Third row: Sheila Brooks, -?-, Daisy Gritton, -?-, Annie Norton, Muriel Thomas, -?-, Vera Lester, Muriel Slater. Second row: -?-, -?-, -?-, Enid Harrison, -?-, -?-, Dolly Boden, Rosie Jay, -?-, Front row: -?-, -?-, Betty Atkins, Bessie Milner, -?-.

Bent Street Infants' School concert, *c.* 1927. Back row, left to right: -?-, -?-, Denys Joanson, George Pearson, Jack Lovett, -?-, -?-, Beryl Vickers. Second row: -?-, -?-, -?-, Brian Evans, -?-, -?-, Dorothy Harris. Front row: -?-, Mildred Page, Muriel Murray.

A class at Bent Street Infants' School, *c.* 1926. Teachers at back, left to right: Miss Lavender, Miss Anslow (Head). Right-hand column of pupils from the front: Brian Evans, Muriel Murray, Tom Willetts, George Pearson.

A class at Moor Street Board School, c. 1902. Vernon Oliver is on the right of the board. The school was closed in about 1930 and the headmaster, Mr Bert Jones, transferred to Brockmoor Junior Mixed School. The Moor Street buildings were acquired by Marsh & Baxter Ltd.

The old toll house at Brettell Lane on the corner of Dennis Hall Road, 1960. This was near the tunnel which carried the tramway from Nagersfield Colliery to George King Harrison's works on Brettell Lane.

Mr William Baker's Swan Inn at Buckpool where a meeting was held in 1854 to recruit miners for the Hudson's Bay Company mines on Vancouver Island. Twenty-four local men contracted to go and embarked with their families on the barque the *Princess Royal* at London on 2 June 1854. The journey took nearly six months.

The Swan Inn, *c.* 1960. This was a Smith's house, situated in Moor Lane just west of the railway line.

The Vine Inn, known locally as The Bull and Bladder, and Batham's Brewery near Delph Road and Delph Corner, 1977. Morris dancers are performing outside.

A parade of Brierley Hill British Legion from their club in Albion Street for a service of dedication of a new women's standard at Brockmoor Church by the Revd R.D. Payne, 1962. The group is in Bank Street, with the Civic Buildings in the background, and includes in the middle row: Mrs Winifred Jarvis (Women's Section secretary), Mrs Sayce (standard bearer), Mrs Vera Chadwick and Mr Davies on the pavement.

John Corbett (1817–1901) was born in Gas Street, Delph, and worked in his father's canal haulage business from 1828 until 1840, when he entered engineering. He bought Salt Prior Salt Works, Droitwich, in 1852 and turned it into a very profitable business, increasing production eightfold. A good employer, a benefactor to many churches, he built the Chateau Impney just outside Droitwich, and was an MP for Droitwich (later Mid Worcs) from 1874 to 1892.

Colour Sergeant Anthony Booth VC served with the 80th Staffordshire Volunteers from 1864 to 1898, and won the VC in an action against the Zulus on the Intombi River in 1879. He completed his service with the Brierley Hill Volunteers, 'C' Company, 1st Battalion, the South Staffordshire Regiment, in 1898, died in 1899, and was buried in St Michael's churchyard on 12 December 1899.

Brierley Hill giant, George Lovatt, born in 1869, and seen here in the late 1920s. He weighed over 40 stone and his coffin had to be lowered from his bedroom at Round Oak. Special equipment was used for his interment at St Michael's churchyard on 16 March 1933.

Harold Thompson, 1962. He was a familiar figure in the Delph area for nearly 30 years. Sometimes he carried a violin which he played from time to time. His favourite tune was 'I Dreamt I Dwelt in Marble Halls'. He often slept in a brickyard or nearby stable, and died in 1974; local people raised money for his funeral.

Stan Harley joined the 1st Battalion the Worcestershire Regiment in 1914, when only 15 years old. He won the DCM in France and returned to Round Oak Works in 1919. This photograph of him in full military gear dates from 1921, and was one of a series used by monumental masons George Brown and Sons of Kidderminster for the figure on the war memorial.

The war memorial on Church Hill.

Baruch Beckley, founder of Beckley's Garage, Dudley Road, in 1888, seen here adjusting a Rex motorcycle, 1908. The small boy is Baruch Beckley's son Frank, aged 7, who became a partner in the business, retiring in 1962. Will Cartwright is mending the puncture. The garage had strong connections with the town fire brigade and ambulance.

Sunbeam Cycle Works of Wolverhampton awarded the coveted 'Certificate of Agency' to Baruch Beckley in 1898.

Charles William Gripton of West Bromwich became Foreman of the LNWR (later LMS) Canal Depot at Nine Locks Wharf after service at Kidderminster, where he met his wife. He is seen here in a gig in the 1920s ready to carry the LMS agent to other LMS outposts at the Bonded Warehouse and Dadford's Wharf.

Ray Westwood, left, in action for Bolton Wanderers, 1930s. He was born in Brierley Hill in 1912, captained the town schoolboys' team when aged 12, and played for Stourbridge Town Reserves and Brierley Hill Alliance before signing for Bolton in 1928. He played for England in 1934 with Stanley Matthews, and in 15 representative matches. At the end of his football career Ray bought a newsagent's shop in Fenton Street. He died in 1982.

A scrapbook competition at the Children's Library, judged by Mr H.W. Woodward (Librarian) and Miss I.C. Horton (Children's Librarian), 1965. The prize-winners, left to right, are Lesley Adams, Elaine Roseblade, Gail Workman, Jane Stringer, Sheena Ward, Rosemary Johnson and Mary Walker. In 1966 Mr Woodward, who started the local glass collection, became Inspector of Dudley's Libraries and later Keeper of the Glass. The collection has since developed into the world-famous Broadfield House Museum of Glass.

The monorail which links various parts of the Merry Hill-Waterfront complex, 1990s.

Brierley Hill and District Schools Football Team, 1951. Standing, left to right: Mr Richard R. Dews, Timmins, -?-, Harris, -?-, Wooldridge, -?-, Mr F. Phipps, Weston. Seated: Worton, Cochrane, Smith, Bagley, Cooper. The team, finalists in the English Schools Shield, drew 2–2 at Molyneux and lost the second leg 3–1 at Goodison Park.

Brierley Hill, Sedgley and Tipton Schools Football Team 1959. Standing, left to right: Nicklin, Rushton, Sproson, Jefferies, Green, Cotterill, Hartland. Second row: Edwards, Ash, Baker, Hill, Page, Kendrick, Attwood. Front row: -?-, Grainger. The team, joint holders of the English Schools Shield, defeated Doncaster 2–0 at Molyneux and lost 2–0 in the second leg at Doncaster.

Section Two

BROCKMOOR

By 1840 the need for a church for the growing population led to a petition to the
Ecclesiastical Commissioners for England to set up a separate district for Brockmoor, and
this was accepted on 3 September 1844. Two acres of land and a dwelling house were
conveyed to the Commissioners by the Earl of Dudley for the building of a new church and
a parsonage. The church was consecrated as St John's on 11 December 1845.

The Revd R.D. Payne, Brockmoor's tenth incumbent, 1963. During his first three years as vicar, much-needed repair work on the church was carried out.

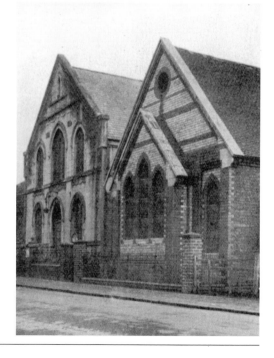

Brockmoor Wesleyan Methodist Chapel and schoolroom, late 1920s. Built on what was known as 'The Sandhole', the chapel was purchased in 1838 from William Beckley. The schoolroom was added in 1886, and the chapel was rebuilt in 1898. The congregation joined others and transferred to the new Methodist Church in Bank Street, Brierley Hill, in 1971.

Brockmoor Primary School, Station Road, Brockmoor, built as a Kingswinford Board School in 1887, and demolished in 1995 after a new £2 million school had opened behind it. On adjoining sites an infants' school was built in 1910 and a senior girls' school in the early 1930s.

May Day activity in Brockmoor School playground, *c.* 1922. The Boat Inn was on an unmade road. The houses top right are on Station Road.

The Scholarship class at Brockmoor Junior Mixed School, 1932. Seated, left to right: Stanley Philpott, Betty Benton, Cliff Bridgens, Harden Catwright, Eileen Hill, Keith Jones. Standing: Jack Dutton, Jack Turner. Their teacher was Mr Bert Jones.

The Boat Inn on what is now Pheasant Street, 1920s.

The Bottle and Glass in 1980, just before its removal to the Black Country Museum where it has been perfectly reconstructed. Situated almost opposite the Moor Lane–Leys Road junction it backed on to a canal, as it does in its new location. Built in about 1800, it had two rooms for drinkers (a small wood-lined room and a bar), a kitchen at the back and two upstairs rooms.

The Brockmoor House Inn on the corner of Station Road and High Street, Brockmoor, c. 1912. The building was propped up because of subsidence caused by the operations of a nearby pit. A new inn of the same name stands on the opposite corner of Station Road and High Street.

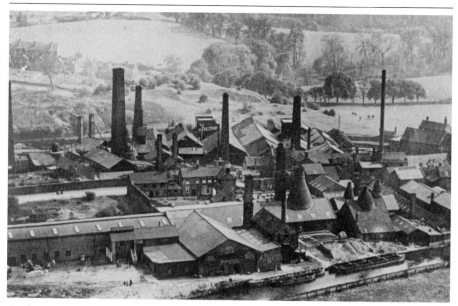

Carder's Pottery on Leys Road, bordering the canal, late 19th century. Beyond is an ironworks and, slightly further down the road, Eagle Foundry. It was at the pottery that Fred Carder's terracotta panels for Wordsley Art School were fired. In the distance can be seen cottages in Moor Lane.

Some of the original chimneys at Baldwin's Cookley Works, from the railway line, *c.* 1950.

An old bridge across the Fens branch of the Stourbridge Canal near Baldwin's Cookley works, early 1950s. In 1885 John Knight transferred his puddling furnaces, rolling mill and tin and terne coating plant from Cookley near Kidderminster to Brockmoor. In 1902 it was taken over by Baldwin's, which in 1945 joined a South Wales firm, Richard Thomas.

The new bridge which was constructed to allow huge works extensions on the north side of the canal, 1956. Over 1,400 people were employed at the Brockmoor works at one time. Fewer than a hundred now operate a modern highly automated plant to coat strip steel continuously.

The entrance to what remains of the former Richard Thomas and Baldwin's premises, the CRM Depot of British Steel, 1966.

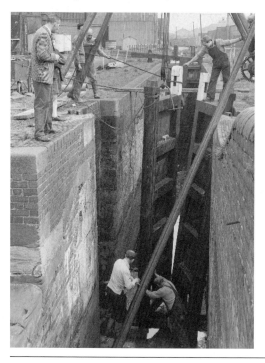

Lock renewal at Buckpool, 1965.

Section Three

KINGSWINFORD & WALL HEATH

St Mary's Church, c. 1960. Parts of the tower date back to the 11th century. It remained the church for the huge parish of Kingswinford until it was threatened by mining activities; Holy Trinity Church, Wordsley, was built in 1831 to replace it. St Mary's Church reopened in 1846 to cater for a smaller parish.

The tympanum over the door of the vestry depicts a contest between St Michael and Satan, and is thought to have been carved by stonemasons who had previously worked on Norman castles in about 1120.

St Mary's Church seen from across The Village, late 19th century.

The original St Mary's School, built in 1835 near Bradley Hall. It was demolished in the 1970s, a new school in Queen Street replacing it.

The Court House, facing The Village, *c.* 1910.

The land for Kingswinford Wesleyan Methodist Church was purchased from Edward Addenbrooke in 1848 and opened for services in 1853. Improvements were carried out in 1870, 1903 and 1923. In 1873 Thomas Woodall, famous glass decorator,was appointed organist. The last service there was held on 12 June 1966. The Sunday School site was bought by the post office and a new sorting office built. Methodism in Kingswinford is now concentrated at the Stream Road church, which opened on 18 June 1966.

The old Toll House, built to conform with 18th-century Acts of Parliament, at the junction of Bromley Lane and Stream Road. In more recent times the occupier supplied passing tram crews with jugs of tea.

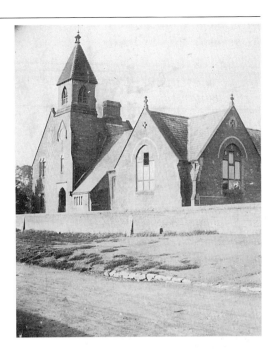

The Glynne School, Cot Lane, *c*. 1920. Originally a church school founded in 1857 on land donated by Sir Richard Glynne, when the Oak Farm Company collapsed and the associated school closed. Holy Trinity Church was involved with both, but in 1902 The Glynne, now a primary school, passed to local education authority control.

Market Street, looking towards The Cross, *c*. 1900. On the left is the post office, a fruiterer and Woodall's shop, later an outlet for the glass creations of George Woodall (1850–1925) who lived on the premises, now a Trustee Savings Bank branch. The Vine Inn is middle left.

Market Street, looking towards The Cross, 1940s. The Grand Cinema is on the left, converted from the old Market Hall and operated as a cinema until 1964. On the right is the Market Hall Tavern, a home-brew inn run by Dick Chambers and later Cliff, his son.

Shops in Market Street opposite the Market Hall, looking towards The Cross, *c.* 1910. The Wesleyan Methodist Church is visible.

Bradley Hall, a fine timbered building on Dudley Road, early 1920s. Thought to be the home of a yeoman family named Bradley, the house is dated 1596. The last occupant was Henry Webb, farmer and butcher. The old hall was sold for £2,775, dismantled by Messrs A.H. Guest and re-erected as Bradley Lodge at Stratford-on-Avon in 1925, under the aegis of the Bromsgrove Guild of Craftsmen.

The rear of Summerhill Court on the corner of Cot Lane and Lodge Lane, c. 1920. A Mr Druller was head gardener and lived in the lodge. The Court was demolished in the early 1990s.

Summerhill, on the corner of Swindon Road and Summerhill, photographed by George Woodall, *c.* 1910. It was once the home of Sir Sidney Barratt, chairman of the Oldbury-based company Albright and Wilson. It is now the Summerhill House Hotel.

The army camp at the top of Bromley Lane, late 1940s. After the Second World War it accommodated prisoners of war.

Mrs Rushton's general store, High Street, *c.* 1900. Left to right: Mrs Mary Ann Rushton (owner), Mrs Jane Powell (owner's daughter), Miss Elsie Rushton, Mrs Polly Thatcher (of Penzer Street).

Wall Heath Church of the Ascension, built in about 1893.

Wall Heath School, built of blue bricks in about 1851. The Infants' School to the left was built in 1910 and is now used as a private nursery. The new Church of the Ascension Primary School was built to the right of the building shown here, which was then demolished.

A class at Wall Heath School, *c.* 1918. Mr Clewley (headmaster) is on the right and Mr Roberts (deputy) is on the left. Mary Parkes of Enville Road is in the middle of the front row.

A 'gym' class at Wall Heath School, with Miss Phoebe Wood who later taught at Penzer Street Senior School, *c.* 1920. Mary Parkes is third from right in the front row.

A physical training class at Wall Heath School with Miss Phoebe Wood, 1920s.

Holbeche House, 1920s. This was part of the Earl of Dudley's Estate, and was auctioned in 1947. In 1605 Stephen Lyttelton lived here. He was a friend of Robert Catesby, one of the principal Gunpowder Plotters, and when Guy Fawkes was arrested some of the conspirators fled to Holbeche House where they made their last stand. Catesby and three conspirators were killed. Lyttelton escaped but was captured at Prestwood, charged with high treason at Worcester and hanged.

The original Yew Tree Inn, Enville Road, is thought to have been built in the 1840s. Occupants included people named Taylor, Ann Bradley, Aston, Waterfield, and then in 1919 Alec Mason – who developed the property into an attraction which drew parties from a wide area.

The Pleasure Gardens at Yew Tree Hotel, c. 1920. The inn was modernised and Alec Mason, who had trained at Windsor Castle gardens, welcomed visitors who came by horse-drawn coach and later by charabanc. The site was cleared by 1995 and houses were built on it.

The entrance to High Street, Wall Heath, from the south, between the wars. The Earl of Dudley's Pensnett Railway crossed the road near the Wall Heath Inn, en route to Ashwood Basin off the Staffordshire–Worcestershire Canal.

This glass sculpture was a gift from Fred Carder of Corning, USA, in 1958 to Brierley Hill Rotary Club. It is on loan to Broadfield House Glass Museum.

Section Four

PENSNETT

The Church of St Mark was built between 1846 and 1849 on the steep slope of Barrow Hill at a total cost of £13,000, including furnishings. Lord Ward was made a patron as he met half of the costs. It soon became a parish with a vicar.

The Wesleyan Chapel at Bromley, 1920s. The land to build the church on was bought in 1828. A Sunday School was added in 1848 and it is thought that this was let for use as a Dame School.

The Independent Methodist Church at Pensnett, *c.* 1944. Primitive Methodists at Shutt End decided to secede from the Brierley Hill Circuit, and founded an Independent Methodist Church opposite Victoria Road, Commonside. It was opened for worship on 29 July 1894.

Becknell Field Farm, *c.* 1910.

Corbyn's Hall dates back to the 16th century, when the Corbyns were Pensnett gentry. The Gibbons family, iron masters and coal producers, once owned it. By the early 20th century, when this photograph was taken, the building had suffered badly from mining subsidence. It was demolished in 1916.

Standard Two at St Mark's Church of England Primary School, *c*. 1906. Hilda Smith (later Mantle) is in the second row from the front, third left from the right-hand side. James Campbell is on her left. The headmaster is Mr J. Skelding and the class teacher Mrs Sturman.

Elderly Pensnett residents assembled outside Pensnett post office after collecting their first old age pensions (5*s* a week), 1911. At the extreme right is James Pearce, miner, of Chapel Street.

The Plantation, formerly Shutt End House, which stood in 12 acres on Kingswinford Road, 1920s. Built in 1760 it was originally a substantial farmhouse. It was bought in 1915 by Dr H.W. Plant: his family moved in, but his surgery continued to be at Oak House. The Plantation was demolished in the 1960s, and about 40 houses built on the site.

Dr Plant's family at The Plantation, 1941. Standing, left to right: Kathleen ('Bo' – Peter's wife), Peter, Tony (killed at Salerno), Fred (RAMC – captured at St Valery and escaped and awarded the MC), Arthur (practised at Pensnett and Kingswinford), John and his wife Nancy. Front row: Fred's wife Mary ('Muff') and son Peter, Ann, Dr H.W. Plant and grandson Michael, Mrs Plant and grandson David, Mary, Elizabeth.

The Middle Pool, 1920s. The other pools were Grove and Fens. They once served as canal feeders but now are part of a recreational area.

High Street Pensnett, looking towards Kingswinford, 1930s. The post office had moved to the opposite side of the road by this date. A branch of Dudley Co-operative Society opened in 1929.

QUARRY BANK

Amelia, Baroness Ward, laid the first stone at Quarry Bank parish church on 28 October
1845, and the church was consecrated in March 1847. A £500 grant towards the cost
came from the £1 million fund set up by Queen Victoria, and Stourbridge Canal Company
donated £25. The firebricks with which the church is built came from Messrs Harper &
Moore. A secondhand organ was bought in the 1860s, and this is said to have been
conveyed by canal to a wharf on the Dudley Canal at Nine Locks.

New Street Methodist Church, 1970s. This has now been demolished and houses have been built on the site.

Mount Pleasant Methodist Church opened in 1828 and was built at a cost of £850. A schoolroom was added in 1829 and let for use as a Dame school. The church records show that in 1839 money was spent on ironwork to secure the building, and also to purchase the mineral rights beneath.

For the first time in the history of Quarry Bank parish church, women became 'sidesmen' in March 1976 and kept that title. The ladies include Mesdames Bessie Cranton, Madge Grove, Anne Willetts, Ivy Homer, Jeanne Haywood, Margaret Stiff, Nancy Sidaway, June Grove, Vera White, Vera Bate, and the Vicar, the Revd Victor Irwin.

Dr Francis Maylett Smith with his sister Mabel Crofton at her home in Sussex, 1938. Dr Smith practised in Quarry Bank from 1916 to 1933 at 'Ingleside', High Street, which later became the practice of Drs Rogers and Fair, and is now Quarry Bank Surgery. Dr Smith was stone deaf, and was one of the first Quarry Bank residents to have a car.

Cradley Heath High Street, *c.* 1914. This picture is included as it shows that a firm of solicitors there, Homfray, Holbertson and Mellor, housed the offices of Quarry Bank Urban District Council.

The interior of Noah Bloomer's chainworks in the 1930s.

The war memorial in Quarry Bank Park. In 1919 Ernest Stevens JP, a local manufacturer, gave 18 acres, later increased to 21 acres, for a 'Public Park and Recreation Ground'. The Council made appeals for funds to develop the land as a park and to erect a war memorial. The donor gave another £500. Many unemployed men were engaged on the work and over 500 trees were planted.

The bandstand in Stevens' Park, Quarry Bank, 1930s.

A class at Mount Pleasant Primary School with their teacher, Mrs Hilda Mantle, 1960s. The school was one of the Kingswinford Board Schools opened in 1888. It underwent a huge modernisation and extension programme which was completed in 1992. Mount Pleasant Methodist Church is in the background.

Dunns Bank Football Club, 1976. Back row, left to right: B. Turner, G. Westwood, T. Watts, T. Dingley, D. Dimmock, S. Sidaway, D. Brooks, G. Clews, D. Penn, J. Cartwright, Front row: J. Biddle, D. Undrill, B. Able, G. Knock (captain), M. Dorgan, C. Penn, M. Silitan. The mascot is J. Dingley.

Lower High Street, early 1920s. On the right is Ingleside, doctors' surgery. Further down is the Liberal Club, where a landmine crashed through the roof on 20 December 1940 and did not explode. Another unexploded landmine was found just below the primary school on the left.

Typical late Victorian houses in Victoria Street, looking up towards Coppice Lane.

The Elmar Trio, early 1920s. Percy Beddall of Queen Street emigrated to Australia in 1908, where in 1909 he married Stella Marsden. Their child Elsie was born in 1910. The family developed an 'equilibrist' act for circuses and music halls, the Elmar Trio. They toured India and South Africa before returning to England, where they appeared all over the country until 1932. Elsie married well-known Quarry Bank businessman, Jack Genner, and died in 1987.

Section Six

WORDSLEY

Holy Trinity Church, Wordsley. St Mary's Church, Kingswinford, was too far from growing centres of population in the parish and other churches were needed. In addition the ancient church was threatened by mining operations.. The Earl of Dudley offered a site for a new church on the east side of the main road at Wordsley, and building started in 1829; the architect was Louis Vulliamy. Holy Trinity Church was consecrated in 1831, Kingswinford church closed (reopened 1848), and the Wordsley church became Kingswinford parish church. The National School, now the Church Hall, was built in 1842.

A view of Holy Trinity Church from the south, *c.* 1920. Wordsley Art School is in the centre.

Wordsley Methodist Church, New Street, *c.* 1928. Foundation stones were laid by three Wordsley residents on 16 June 1882: Mrs C. Blackshaw, Mrs W. Davies and Mrs G. Bourne.

Wordsley Girl Guides before their Armistice Day Parade, behind the Church Hall, 1943. Back row, left to right: Janet Fasey, Ann Cadman, Ann Green, Valerie Kay, Leader Violet Walker, -?-, -?-. Third row: -?-, -?-, Brenda Jones, ? Garbett, Audrey Jones, -?-, -?-. Second row: Iris Tandle, Maureen Hingley, -?-, -?-, -?-, -?-, -?-, -?-. Front row: -?-, -?-, Marjorie Walker, -?-, -?-.

The Rectory, *c*. 1920.

Wordsley School of Art, *c.* 1900. This opened in 1899 following a campaign by local glass manufacturers with a long-term view of educating their employees to improve products in order to meet growing international competition. The other half was opened in 1909.

GLASS MANUFACTURE.

A Special Class in this subject is held on Mondays. The Course includes – Composition of Glass generally—Modes of Manufacture—Special properties of Glass—Construction of Furnaces, &c.—Chemical Changes during Manufacture—Composition of Materials used, including colours—Moulds and Tools—Various Methods of Decoration, &c., &c.

The above Syllabus is both *theoretical* and *practical*, and is divided into three grades—Preliminary, Ordinary, and Honours. It is designed to cover the ground of the City and Guilds of London Institute. In the Honours Grade students are expected to possess some knowledge of design, and to attend a class on that subject.

Special attention will be given to Continental methods of work, as studied by the Instructor during the past vacation in Germany and Austria.

Mondays, Preliminary and Ordinary,
7-30 to 9-30.

Honours, 7-30 to 10 p.m.

FEES .. .. .. 2s. 6d.; and Honours, 5s.

Money Prizes, value £4, and Medals are offered by the City and Guilds; and Free Studentships (Money Prizes, value £3, £2, £1), by the Staffs. County Council.

Instructor ... F. CARDER.

E.   R.

. WORDSLEY .

School ✦ of ✦ Art,

(SESSION 1902-3)

Commencing Monday, September 29th.

SUBJECTS :—

Art :

Elementary—Tuesdays and Fridays .. ⎫ 7·15
Advanced—Tuesdays, . Wednesdays, ⎬ to
    and Fridays .. .. ⎭ 9-15.
Morning Classes—Wednesdays . and ⎫ 10-30 to
    Fridays .. .. ⎭ 12-30.

Science :

Geometry and Mechanical Drawing— ⎫ 7·15
    Mondays .. .. ⎬ to
TECHNICAL SUBJECTS : ⎪ 9-15.
Glass Manufacture—Mondays.. .. ⎭

STAFF —

*Art Master :—*F. CARDER, Gold Medallist
*Assistants :—*Misses E. & M. A. RICHARDSON, and N. WILKES.
*Science Master :—*B. F. MASON.
*Glass Manufacture :—*F. CARDER.

Hon. Secs. : ⎱ **W. NORTHWOOD,**
     ⎰ **C. DUDLEY.**

Prospectus for the School of Art, 1902–3, when the art master was Frederick Carder. It was his last year there before he emigrated to the USA in 1903. A party from the American Carder Society visited the area in 1994.

The complete Art School, which has not been used since the Community Association moved to new premises at The Green. Note the four terracotta panels on the first floor, designed by Frederick Carder and his brother George. They were stolen in 1993.

The Carder family, *c.* 1895. The children are Stanley (who died in 1899), Cyril in a dress (usual at that time) and Gladys. The Carders lived in John Street, and Frederick was a glass designer at Stevens & Williams, Brierley Hill.

A party from the School of Art on a trip to Bewdley, 1903. Frederick Carder is seated on the left, and on his left is his daughter Gladys. Behind her is Mrs Annie Carder with hands clasped. Son Cyril is immediately in front of his father.

Looking down High Street, Wordsley, before tram lines were laid.

A view south from Cooknall, *c.* 1920. The glass kilns of Albert Glass Works, Red House Glass Works, White House Glass Works and Richardson can be seen. Webbs Seed Works is in the middle.

A photograph looking down the Stourbridge '16' locks towards Dadford's Warehouse and Stuart's glass cone beyond, 1976.

The Board Room at Wordsley Hospital, 1972. This was built in 1861 to serve the Union Workhouse which took inmates from a wide area and which was administered by The Board of Guardians. It became the Stourbridge Union Workhouse and £3,950 was spent on buildings in 1837. During the First World War part of it was used as a military hospital, and in the Second World War an American Army plastic surgery unit was based here. After the creation of the National Health Service a large range of hospital services developed on the site.

The house where Charles II called for refreshment in September 1651 after the Battle of Worcester, seen here in the late 1950s. The king journeyed north to Moseley Hall, Boscobel and Bentley Hall before escaping from Shoreham to France. He was restored to the throne in 1660. A modern shop now stands on the site on the corner of High Street and Kinver Street.

Wordsley Hall, *c.* 1900. This was once the home of Ben Richardson, a leading Wordsley glass manufacturer.

This hop warehouse was all that remained in 1990 of a huge Wordsley supplier of seeds. It has now been replaced by houses. William Webb & Sons, founded in 1861, was a large concern whose land for the production of seeds exceeded 17,000 acres, mainly at Wordsley and Kinver. Local names were given to seeds: Wordsley Wonder, Kinver Gem, Electric Light, Culverwell's Telegraph (peas), Kinver Monarch, Wordsley Queen, Stourbridge Glory (potatoes). An 1889 catalogue describes the firm as 'The Queen's Seedsmen'. Wordsley Garden Centre on part of the original site is a reminder of this famous local firm.

Brook Street School, 1975. It ceased being a school when Audnam Secondary School moved to the new Buckpool School in Brierley Hill Road, and Brook Primary took over the old secondary school premises at the top of George Street.

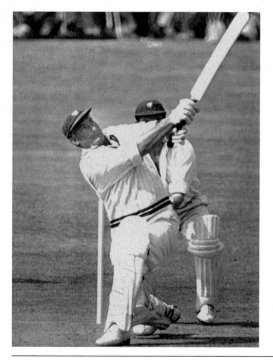

Wordsley Test cricketer, Don Kenyon, scoring a six against Somerset at Kidderminster, *c*. 1960. He registered for Worcestershire in 1939, played several representative matches while serving in the RAF and played continuously for the county until he retired in 1967 after being captain from 1959. He played for England eight times, was a Test selector and was appointed President of Worcestershire CCC in 1986.

The former Peacock Inn still stands in Kinver Street, and was photographed earlier this century.

Gill's butcher's shop just below the Cat Inn, *c.* 1905. Ezra Gill set up the shop in the late 1890s. On the left is Hannah Gill with Edith Whitehouse, her mother.

Acknowledgements

Eileen Bailey • Graham Beckley • Dr Peter Bloore • V. Charles Booth
Jim Boulton • Dr Paul Collins • Denis H. Crofton • Betty Dix • Patricia Dunn Charles
J.L. Elwell • R.E.G. Evers • Kevin Gripton • Alison Grove
H. Jack Haden • Mrs. S. Haden • Jean M. Hill • Eileen E. Hobbs
Lawrence Hollis • Jo Hunt • Ray James • Winifred Jarvis • Keith Jeavons
Barbara Julian • Don Kenyon • Hilda Mantle • John Marsh
Michael Mensing • R.O.C. Mellor • David Newton • George Pearson
Mary Pearson • George Philpott • Dr Arthur Plant • Frank Power
Dr Trevor Raybould • Eric Richardson • L. Jack Roberts • Madeline Sharratt
Bert Shaw • P.J. Shoesmith • John Sparry • Pearl Taylor
Arthur Thompson • Eric Timmins • Janet Tomlinson • Bert Turley
Geoff Warburton • Dr John West • Joan White • Fred Willetts • Ned Williams H.W.
Woodward • Anthony O. Wright • Aerofilms • Black Country Society *Bolton Evening
News* • Brierley Hill Printing Company • Brierley Hill Library British Steel
(Brockmoor) • Broadfield House Museum of Glass
Corning Museum of Glass • Dudley Metropolitan Borough • *Express & Star*
'Hal' of Stourbridge • Midland News Association
Richardson Developments
Stourbridge News & County Express.

Every effort has been made to contact copyright holders of photographs where
copyright has not originated from those who own them.

THE BLACK COUNTRY SOCIETY

This voluntary society, affiliated to the Civic Trust, was founded in 1967 as a reaction to the trend of the late 1950s and early 1960s to amalgamate everything into large units and in the Midlands to sweep away the area's industrial heritage in the process.

The general aim of the Society is to create interest in the past, present and future of the Black Country, and early on it campaigned for the establishment of an industrial museum. In 1975 the Black Country Museum was started by Dudley Borough Council on 26 acres of totally derelict land adjoining the grounds of Dudley Castle. This has developed into an award-winning museum which attracts over 250,000 visitors annually.

There are over two thousand members of the Black Country Society and all receive the quarterly magazine *The Blackcountryman*, of which over 112 issues have been published since its founding in 1967. In the whole collection there are some 1,700 authoritative articles on all aspects of the Black Country by historians, teachers, researchers, students, subject experts and ordinary folk with an extraordinary story to tell. The whole constitutes a unique resource about the area and is a mine of information for students and researchers who frequently refer to it. Many schools and libraries are subscribers. Three thousand copies of the magazine are printed each quarter. It is non-commercial, and contributors do not receive payment for their articles.

PO Box 71 · Kingswinford · West Midlands DY6 9YN

BRITAIN IN OLD PHOTOGRAPHS

To order any of these titles please telephone Littlehampton Book Services on 01903 721596

ALDERNEY

Alderney: A Second Selection, *B Bonnard*

BEDFORDSHIRE

Bedfordshire at Work, *N Lutt*

BERKSHIRE

Maidenhead, *M Hayles & D Hedges*
Around Maidenhead, *M Hayles & B Hedges*
Reading, *P Southerton*
Reading: A Second Selection, *P Southerton*
Sandhurst and Crowthorne, *K Dancy*
Around Slough, *J Hunter & K Hunter*
Around Thatcham, *P Allen*
Around Windsor, *B Hedges*

BUCKINGHAMSHIRE

Buckingham and District, *R Cook*
High Wycombe, *R Goodearl*
Around Stony Stratford, *A Lambert*

CHESHIRE

Cheshire Railways, *M Hitches*
Chester, *S Nichols*

CLWYD

Clwyd Railways, *M Hitches*

CLYDESDALE

Clydesdale, *Lesmahagow Parish Historical Association*

CORNWALL

Cornish Coast, *T Bowden*
Falmouth, *P Gilson*
Lower Fal, *P Gilson*
Around Padstow, *M McCarthy*
Around Penzance, *J Holmes*
Penzance and Newlyn, *J Holmes*
Around Truro, *A Lyne*
Upper Fal, *P Gilson*

CUMBERLAND

Cockermouth and District, *J Bernard Bradbury*
Keswick and the Central Lakes, *J Marsh*
Around Penrith, *F Boyd*
Around Whitehaven, *H Fancy*

DERBYSHIRE

Derby, *D Buxton*
Around Matlock, *D Barton*

DEVON

Colyton and Seaton, *T Gosling*
Dawlish and Teignmouth, *G Gosling*
Devon Aerodromes, *K Saunders*
Exeter, *P Thomas*
Exmouth and Budleigh Salterton, *T Gosling*
From Haldon to Mid-Dartmoor, *T Hall*
Honiton and the Otter Valley, *J Yallop*
Around Kingsbridge, *K Tanner*
Around Seaton and Sidmouth, *T Gosling*
Seaton, Axminster and Lyme Regis, *T Gosling*

DORSET

Around Blandford Forum, *B Cox*
Bournemouth, *M Colman*
Bridport and the Bride Valley, *J Burrell & S Humphries*
Dorchester, *T Gosling*
Around Gillingham, *P Crocker*

DURHAM

Darlington, *G Flynn*
Darlington: A Second Selection, *G Flynn*
Durham People, *M Richardson*
Houghton-le-Spring and Hetton-le-Hole, *K Richardson*
Houghton-le-Spring and Hetton-le-Hole:
  A Second Selection, *K Richardson*
Sunderland, *S Miller & B Bell*
Teesdale, *D Coggins*
Teesdale: A Second Selection, *P Raine*
Weardale, *J Crosby*
Weardale: A Second Selection, *J Crosby*

DYFED

Aberystwyth and North Ceredigion,
  Dyfed Cultural Services Dept
Haverfordwest, *Dyfed Cultural Services Dept*
Upper Tywi Valley, *Dyfed Cultural Services Dept*

ESSEX

Around Grays, *B Evans*

GLOUCESTERSHIRE

Along the Avon from Stratford to Tewkesbury, *J Jeremiah*
Cheltenham: A Second Selection, *R Whiting*
Cheltenham at War, *P Gill*
Cirencester, *J Welsford*
Around Cirencester, *E Cuss & P Griffiths*
Forest, The, *D Mullin*
Gloucester, *J Voyce*
Around Gloucester, *A Sutton*
Gloucester: From the Walwin Collection, *J Voyce*
North Cotswolds, *D Viner*
Severn Vale, *A Sutton*
Stonehouse to Painswick, *A Sutton*
Stroud and the Five Valleys, *S Gardiner & L Padin*
Stroud and the Five Valleys: A Second Selection,
  S Gardiner & L Padin
Stroud's Golden Valley, *S Gardiner & L Padin*
Stroudwater and Thames & Severn Canals,
  E Cuss & S Gardiner
Stroudwater and Thames & Severn Canals: A Second
  Selection, *E Cuss & S Gardiner*
Tewkesbury and the Vale of Gloucester, *C Hilton*
Thornbury to Berkeley, *J Hudson*
Uley, Dursley and Cam, *A Sutton*
Wotton-under-Edge to Chipping Sodbury, *A Sutton*

GWYNEDD

Anglesey, *M Hitches*
Gwynedd Railways, *M Hitches*
Around Llandudno, *M Hitches*
Vale of Conwy, *M Hitches*

HAMPSHIRE

Gosport, *J Sadden*
Portsmouth, *P Rogers & D Francis*

HEREFORDSHIRE

Herefordshire, *A Sandford*

HERTFORDSHIRE

Barnet, *I Norrie*
Hitchin, *A Fleck*
St Albans, *S Mullins*
Stevenage, *M Appleton*

ISLE OF MAN

The Tourist Trophy, *B Snelling*

ISLE OF WIGHT

Newport, *D Parr*
Around Ryde, *D Parr*

JERSEY

Jersey: A Third Selection, *R Lemprière*

KENT

Bexley, *M Scott*
Broadstairs and St Peter's, *J Whyman*
Bromley, Keston and Hayes, *M Scott*
Canterbury: A Second Selection, *D Butler*
Chatham and Gillingham, *P MacDougall*
Chatham Dockyard, *P MacDougall*
Deal, *J Broady*
Early Broadstairs and St Peter's, *B Wootton*
East Kent at War, *D Collyer*
Eltham, *J Kennett*
Folkestone: A Second Selection, *A Taylor & E Rooney*
Goudhurst to Tenterden, *A Guilmant*
Gravesend, *R Hiscock*
Around Gravesend, *R Hiscock & D Grierson*
Herne Bay, *J Hawkins*
Lympne Airport, *D Collyer*
Maidstone, *I Hales*
Margate, *R Clements*
RAF Hawkinge, *R Humphreys*
RAF Manston, *RAF Manston History Club*
RAF Manston: A Second Selection,
  RAF Manston History Club
Ramsgate and Thanet Life, *D Perkins*
Romney Marsh, *E Carpenter*
Sandwich, *C Wanostrocht*
Around Tonbridge, *C Bell*
Tunbridge Wells, *M Rowlands & I Beavis*
Tunbridge Wells: A Second Selection,
  M Rowlands & I Beavis
Around Whitstable, *C Court*
Wingham, Adisham and Littlebourne, *M Crane*

LANCASHIRE

Around Barrow-in-Furness, *J Garbutt & J Marsh*
Blackpool, *C Rothwell*
Bury, *J Hudson*
Chorley and District, *J Smith*
Fleetwood, *C Rothwell*
Heywood, *J Hudson*
Around Kirkham, *C Rothwell*
Lancashire North of the Sands, *J Garbutt & J Marsh*
Around Lancaster, *S Ashworth*
Lytham St Anne's, *C Rothwell*
North Fylde, *C Rothwell*
Radcliffe, *J Hudson*
Rossendale, *B Moore & N Dunnachie*

LEICESTERSHIRE

Around Ashby-de-la-Zouch, *K Hillier*
Charnwood Forest, *I Keil, W Humphrey & D Wix*
Leicester, *D Burton*
Leicester: A Second Selection, *D Burton*
Melton Mowbray, *T Hickman*
Around Melton Mowbray, *T Hickman*
River Soar, *D Wix, P Shacklock & I Keil*
Rutland, *T Clough*
Vale of Belvoir, *T Hickman*
Around the Welland Valley, *S Mastoris*

LINCOLNSHIRE

Grimsby, *J Tierney*
Around Grimsby, *J Tierney*
Grimsby Docks, *J Tierney*
Lincoln, *D Cuppleditch*